The Sorrow of Nature

The Way of the Cross
with
George Congreve SSJE and St Thérèse of Lisieux

Luke Miller, Archdeacon of Hampstead

The Messenger of the Catholic League
NUMBER 296 • Special Edition, January 2014

© The Catholic League 2014

First published 2014 by the Catholic League

www.unitas.org.uk

ISBN: 978-0-9928497-0-2

Digitally printed by Parchments of Oxford

Printworks, Crescent Road, Cowley, Oxford, England OX4 2PB

email: print@parchmentUK.com   www.ParchmentUK.com

Contents

Foreword

The Catholic League was established in 1913 to promote and strive for the corporate reunion of the Church of England and the Catholic Church, through complete communion in the Catholic faith with the successor of Peter in the Apostolic See of Rome. A hundred years later it is an ecumenical society founded on Catholic ecumenical principle, working and praying for the institutional communion of the Anglican and Catholic Churches and the reconciliation of English Christianity.

Its co-founder, Fr Henry Joy Fynes-Clinton, was a close friend and collaborator of Fr Alfred Hope Patten, the vicar of Walsingham who re-founded the Anglican Shrine on the same principle. The League was the first body to collect funds in support of the restoration of the Holy House and among the first to organise a pilgrimage to venerate the restored image of Our Lady of Walsingham. The Fynes-Clinton Chantry is also the Anglican chapel for the Catholic League, dedicated to Our Lady of Victories as Mother of the Church and as defender and advocate of its Catholic unity with Peter in Christ.

In preparation for the League's centenary, members of the League retraced the steps of the founders to make a pilgrimage of thanksgiving and hope: thanksgiving for the friendship, mutual understanding, constructive dialogue, spiritual solidarity and pastoral cooperation that has grown among Anglicans and Catholics in the last hundred years; and hope that, whatever the differences and divergences between the Church of England and the Catholic Church with regard to both faith and order that have magnified in recent times, despite our theological dialogue and good ecclesial friendship, nonetheless the Lord's prayer for our unity will be fulfilled, and that the Sovereign

Father will grant us all the grace of fullness of communion in one faith and life, one Bread and one Body, "according to his will, according to his means" (Paul Couturier).

There could have been no better spiritual guide for us than Fr Luke Miller, Archdeacon of Hampstead. Comparing the writings of St Thérèse of Lisieux and of Fr George Congreve SSJE, a Cowley Father who in his day was one of the great figures in the spiritual life of the Church of England and whose works and significance deserve to be rediscovered, Fr Miller showed us how, in different parts of the Church and unknown to each other, strikingly similar mystical insights once stirred an Anglican and a Roman Catholic alike to closer union with our Lord. In the spirit of this common spiritual heritage, itself a living instance of the unity for which we pray, Fr Luke drew deeper on Fr Congreve's thoughts to take us, station by station, to the very foot of the Cross.

We are very grateful to Fr Miller for enabling us to collect the talks to inspire a wider audience with their spiritual ecumenism, and we commend the Stations of the Cross that conclude them, not only for deeper devotion in this Lent during our hundredth year, but also so that together, as Paul Couturier put it, we may enter with Christ into His suffering of our separation, allow His prayer to penetrate within us, take possession of us and ascend us to union with His Father.

Mark Woodruff
Priest Director of the the Catholic League

December 2013

George Congreve SSJE

George Congreve, scion of a notable Irish Anglican Cavalier family and a relative of the Restoration playwright William Congreve, gave up his curacy, responding to a vocation to be a missionary. In 1872 he presented himself to Fr Richard Meux Benson, founder of the Mission Priests of the Society of St John the Evangelist in Cowley, East Oxford. After several months of being left to his own devices, he asked Benson when his training would begin, only to be told that it was already under way, because it was only a person who had grown holy in constant prayer who could truly be a missionary and convert people to the love of the living God. His vocation turned out to be one of writing and giving retreats both in Cowley and around the British Isles.

The life of the foreign missionary was not to be Congreve's, although he made two trips abroad. First in 1893 he went to Cape Town where there were problems in the Society's House which he helped to sort out, returning "the long way", via Ceylon, Poona, Calcutta and Bombay. In 1899 there were again problems in Cape Town and Congreve sailed in August. He remained in South Africa throughout the Boer War (in which his nephew Walter won a VC) and finally sailed to arrive home in September 1904. It was in this period that the letters and papers which became *The Spiritual Order* and that I have drawn on for these addresses were written.

His publications of sermon and retreat addresses were numerous and in his day he was well known, contributing also many prefaces and introductions to books. Towards the end of his life he worked with Fr William Longridge SSJE, one of the greatest exponents of the Spiritual Exercises of St Ignatius Loyola, to collect Fr Benson's letters.

By the end of his life he was the much loved patriarch of the Society, though never its Superior, with his books and devotional materials achieving the Mission he knew he had been called to decades before - not in a faraway place, but at home and all over the world.

Luke Miller
Archdeacon of Hampstead

Three Talks to the Catholic League

Centenary Pilgrimage
to Our Lady of Walsingham
March 2013

Fr Luke Miller, Archdeacon of Hampstead

1 The Little Way and The Interior Life

On our way to the Cross, I want to share with you the contrasts and the profound similarities that I have found in the spiritual teachings of two great Christian souls. They lived at about the same time, during the nineteenth century. One is famous all over the world; the other is largely forgotten. You will know at least the outline of the life of Marie Thérèse Martin, whom we know as S. Thérèse of Lisieux. Born in 1873, she entered the enclosed Carmelite convent in Lisieux in Normandy at the age of sixteen. She was dead by the time she was twenty-four. She wrote one book, lots of letters, some poems and prayers, and a play. She was deeply mourned by the small circle of those who knew her, but dead to the world. You know the story: they used to publish an obituary notice so that those who prayed for the soul would have something to go on. Thérèse herself said, "It is good to know something of those with whom we shall spend our heaven." They used her spiritual autobiography, written under obedience as a tool of the spiritual life and never meant to be published. Those who read the document were moved. They printed a few more copies and *L'Histoire d'une Ame* – The Story of Soul - became a publishing sensation. Thérèse is now a Doctor of the Church, and her works are read again and again by scholars, spiritual writers, and, most importantly, by simple souls who seek to serve Christ more nearly in their lives.

Thérèse has been misunderstood as sugary sweet and for vacuous, nineteenth-century French sentimentalism. As I hope we shall see, this is not the case for those who penetrate her teaching. It is summed up in what has been called the Little Way.

Our other teacher on our journey to the foot of the Cross was a contrast to Thérèse in almost all respects. He was also a Religious, but an Anglican and a man. Where Thérèse came from the French *petite bourgeoisie*, George Congreve was born into a grand Anglo-Irish family in 1835. One of his ancestors was the poet and playwright, William Congreve; but the others were mainly military: his great-grandfather invented the Congreve Rocket, from which modern ballistic missiles trace their ancestry; his nephew was a General, and his great nephew also a soldier, who together remain the only father and son ever both to win Victoria Crosses. George Congreve joined the Society of S. John the Evangelist, the Cowley Fathers, at Cowley S. John under Fr Richard Meux Benson. He wrote many books and papers over the years of a long life. At the beginning Fr Congreve wanted to be an active missionary and went to Cowley, as he thought, to be trained. In a letter from towards the end of his long life, Congreve wrote how he had been depressed, because the training he had been getting for mission work was not happening. Benson took him for a walk. The Father Founder told the young Congreve that the place to start in mission work to others is in one's own soul. Years later, Congreve wrote that Benson had explained to him:

> We do not come into our Community primarily in order to convert others, but rather with the desire, first of all, to be converted ourselves. Then, if by God's grace we are converted to Him, He may use us in missionary work, or in any other way that He pleases.

He went on:

> Christ's call to the Church to preach the Gospel to every creature had lately reached me and many others with new emphasis; but here I awoke to the urgency of another call, which made even more serious demands than the call to be a

2

missionary: is there some change in myself that I need to make before God can use me in converting others? I had expected that at Cowley we should study theology, improve in methods of teaching, and advance in missionary interest and zeal. But here at Cowley I discovered were men associated for life with the project of promoting their own personal conversion, and of helping one another to live a converted life. To know God and to walk with God seemed to them enough to live for, for out of this relation all their various interests and activities were to grow. Their personal surrender to God was the primary end of their institute; the work they were called to do, whatever it might be, did not add completeness to that end. If the work should fail and leave them with God, their end would be attained none the less, and this personal dedication to God was the power by which they strengthened their hands to go on a mission or to scrub a floor. For most of us there was no opportunity for converting souls, but we were learning to repent of our sins, to obey, to work, and to pray.

Each morning that I rose I remembered there is no preaching for me to-day, no instructing of others, or converting the heathen; but to-day I have to make some advance in my own conversion to God, through whatever work He may give me to do. Here was my first lesson on coming to Cowley. I have not learnt it yet, but I follow on and try still to keep it in view.

Thérèse came to the Carmel at sixteen knowing the same and committing herself to it. In the examination before her Profession, she was asked formally why she had come. Her answer was clear: "I have come to save souls and especially to pray for priests." Congreve ended up travelling all round the country, and to South Africa and

India, as a missionary, but it is Thérèse who is the patron saint of world missions. Who knows which one has converted more souls? Only the Lord knows that; but one would guess that it is the young enclosed nun in her twenty-four years, rather than the active missionary whose span was eighty-eight.

Yet in his day Fr Congreve was very widely known as a guide in the spiritual life. He wrote many books, sermons and papers; and I have had the privilege of reading some of the hundreds of letters which remain in the SSJE archive. He was important in the life of the community, a leader, whilst Thérèse, despite her role as mistress of the novices, was always a junior. Congreve was the person who topped off Bodley's great church of S John the Evangelist at Cowley S. John, but he also reflected deeply on the nature of authority within the Religious life, and the meaning and nature of the vow of obedience. For Thérèse it was enough to be utterly obedient at whatever cost; Congreve faced the reality that obedience must be offered in different directions. I think I may be the only person alive to have read the letter in which Congreve told Benson that enough was enough, and that the Father Founder would have to step aside from leadership of the community, if it was not to collapse.

In my talks, I want to explore some of the other areas in which these two contrasting souls nevertheless teach much the same thing. There seem to me to be enormous areas of overlap, and in their different ways they shed light on each other. I shall focus more on George Congreve, because his work is less well known today and less widely available (although some of his books have been scanned and put up on line). But the Little Flower will help us as well; and it is my thought that, as we meet as Anglican and Roman Catholics, we might be able to learn from these two souls who are so contrasting, yet so much the same.

First, I want to take a paper of Congreve's, entitled *The Interior Life*, and see how it illuminates Thérèse's Little Way.

Congreve begins by contrasting two kinds of Christian life, the outward and the inward. The outward he sees as essentially that of keeping the list of rules, following what is prescribed but without serious engagement. By contrast the Christian following the way of the interior life "lives in the consciousness of a higher world, the world of love, and brings all his business, his interests, and occupation into that new world. It is a world of personal, immediate, vital relation to God." Congreve goes on: "The external Christian, even in saying his prayers, is scoring off a debt: having said them, an obligation is cancelled, he is free until the next prayer time comes … The other, wherever he may be, finds himself in God, makes every fresh start from God, and desires to go with God every step of the way which leads under all circumstances to God."

Congreve goes on to ask whether one might say, "I am a catholic Christian born with an extroverted disposition. Religion always appeals to me in the form of creed, ceremony, rules of conduct, definite external duties. If you speak to me of deliverance from multiplicity into union with God alone, of the soul under law attaining liberty by love, you use phrases that to me have no meaning. I trust that I will have an honest desire to serve God in the only way that I know, *the external way*. Let me follow my own way as the contemplative pursues his, and hope that room might be found for our different ways in another world."

The answer to this is that, since God is one, all ways to Him are the same: "there can only be one way to God and that way is God." Congreve postulates that the external way could and should develop into a more interior life: "The mistake of the external Christian would be to suppose that he must always be external, that his limited attainment is final for him, that he is not meant to know more of God in this world than that He requires him to do his duty. Whereas the new life in any soul is the principle of aspiration, of ever advancing spiritual mastery… every duty done in the grace of God implies a living relation to God, and *that* implies spiritual growth."

Congreve continues this to the logical conclusion: "None of us pretends to *deserve* the light, the power, the interior joy and peace in believing which distinguish the saints; but it would be disloyal to Christ to imagine that our unprogressive state in grace is stereotyped, that we are incapable of a deeper repentance, and a close walk with God than we have yet attained or dreamt of."

Now this echoes directly the language of Thérèse, who famously said that she wanted to be a Saint. In Chapter 4 of *The Story of a Soul* she wrote:

> Our Lord made me understand that the only true glory is that which lasts for ever; and that to attain it there is no necessity to do brilliant deeds, but rather to hide from the eyes of others, and even from oneself, so that "the left hand knows not what the right hand does." Then, as I reflected that I was born for great things, and sought the means to attain them, it was made known to me interiorly that my personal glory would never reveal itself before the eyes of men, but that it would consist in becoming a Saint.

> This aspiration may very well appear rash, seeing how imperfect I was, and am, even now, after so many years of

religious life; yet I still feel the same daring confidence that one day I shall become a great Saint. I am not trusting in my own merits, for I have none; but I trust in Him Who is Virtue and Holiness itself. It is He alone Who, pleased with my feeble efforts, will raise me to Himself, and, by clothing me with His merits, make me a Saint.

To the casual observer, the desire for sanctity is something which seems presumptuous, selfish, ungodly. But Thérèse and Fr Congreve both teach us that it is ungodly not to desire sanctity. Congreve again: "The truest token of divine life in any soul is the desire to advance in grace. And the direction of Christian advance will always be from the outward to the inward, from form to motive, from activity to love."

Thus here we come to the Little Way. Thérèse said that, wanting to be a saint, she was too small to do all the great heroic acts of the great saints. She would look for a direct way, a straight way, a little way. It is the way of love. It means in her teaching letting go of everything except Christ. This of course led her to a profound theology of suffering. To love the other is to let go of the self. There were the childish examples: she described herself as a toy, a ball, a plaything of the Child Jesus; and if He left her to lie unremarked and unplayed with then so much the better.

And there is the much more frightening and adult exposition of what it means to be emptied for Christ, which shines through the other writings. One of these was her poem, *The Unpetalled Rose*. It was written in May 1897, as the tuberculosis which was to kill her that September began to ravage her body. The story is that the poem was written for an elderly sister in another convent. It speaks of the utter seriousness of the interior life: to pray "Thy will be done" and really mean it. It seems to start as the description of a procession at which rose petals are strewn before the Lord; but, "This unpetalled rose is the faithful image, Divine Child, of the heart that wants to sacrifice itself to You unreservedly at each moment."

The flowers are on the altars as decoration, "but I dream of something else: to be unpetalled." The petals which are cast down are just disposed of:

> Jesus for Your love I've squandered my life, my future
> in the eyes of men, a rose forever withered; I must die.

Thérèse said, "to love is to give everything unreservedly. It is to give oneself without any hope of return." When the elderly nun sent a message asking for a final stanza in which the rose is repetalled by Jesus, Thérèse refused: "I don't want to give in order to receive. It is God I love, not myself."

Congreve teaches the same. Our sufferings are the time when we most need God; for our own strength being destroyed, we rely only on Him: "If there are deserts to go through, it is there that we need love's compassion the most."

But neither Fr Congreve nor S. Thérèse teach a dour, sad, sorrowful religion. While they both embrace suffering, they also teach Joy. In her poem, Thérèse says,

> An unpetalled rose gives itself unaffectedly to be no more.
> Like it, with joy I abandon myself to You, Little Jesus.

Indeed for Congreve it is external duty which saps the life of faith of all joy, while the terrible, but wonderful, path of love is filled with rejoicing:

> If there are a few who do the dullest work with radiance of interior joy of the love of God, why should their secret remain hidden from the rest of us? If there are some who give thanks always and for all things, even for pain and loss, why should there not be more?

2 Childhood and Old Age

As infirmity gradually withdraws us from all external work, the question inevitably arises, Has God cut me off from the circulation of the vital charities – the energies of love which are the Church's life? Is there nothing left for me to do for God, for the enormous needs of the world and the church? If I cannot work, or rise from my chair or my bed, love remains to me; I can pray.

George Congreve lived to a ripe old age, even by the standards of today. He died in 1918 aged nearly eighty-three. His last book was a series of meditations on old age, *Treasuries of Hope for the Evening of Life*, from which the above passage is taken. In one of his other books, there is a meditation for a friend's eighty-ninth birthday. In this he beautifully evokes the comparison between the winter days in which nature sleeps, ready to be reborn to new life, with the soul being drawn to a new life:

I by my own fireside am as homeless as the wind without; for *my* winter has come, and *my* evening, which makes all things lonely and strange; and I know no longer this dead world I linger in, from which all are gone who lived with me in that dawn of time, when life was life, eighty years ago. Where is that spring gone, that summer of my life, and the voices of the children that used to come from the garden where my home was, when home was home, long ago?

This silence of my life is no emptiness of mere death, but is rather like the hush of a night in Spring, when the earth is asleep, but dreaming of the new birth which comes tomorrow.

My life grows bare of earthly joys because God is preparing some better thing for me, when I shall be empty enough to receive it; so I am learning to look up and wait for God.

Let the old home fade from my memory, let winter and silent darkness come and blot out all that is lovely in sight and sound and remembrance, in order that in this solitude God may arise upon me, and manifest himself within me, as the eternal abiding Substance of all those reflections of love and beauty that just touched my life with joy in my youth, and passed.

There is much here for our time, in which we all grow so old and the end is perhaps more bitter, because of what they call the long middle, and a man at three score years and ten might expect to be as vigorous as a forty-year-old in times past.

Thérèse also teaches us about death and about age, though she was not yet 25 when she died. More importantly, Congreve takes the idea of Spiritual Childhood that came to Thérèse and turns it round to apply it to old age. He does so implicitly; there were others who did so explicitly. Thérèse was one of four siblings in the Carmel of Lisieux; the others lived to a very great age. Mother Agnes – Pauline, Thérèse's elder sister and godmother - died only in 1951; Celine - Sister Genevieve - died in 1959, having expressly sought to live out the Little Way into her ninetieth year.

Thérèse came from a culture which spoke easily of death and the convent was even more a place where death was treated as the gateway to life. The notes of conversations taken at the deathbeds both of Thérèse and, more than sixty years later, of Sr Genevieve betray a wonderfully shocking openness and simplicity about the coming of death. "We were talking about dates," reports one of the notes; but Thérèse said, "Don't let's talk about it. I have been disappointed so many times."

There was also the context of Carmelite spirituality. Thérèse said, "I no longer have any great desires except that of loving to the point of dying of love." S. John of the Cross had taught this "Death of Love". It is a profound meditation on Jesus, whose death - abandoned by His friends, scorned by all - was consummated when He cried out those terrible words, "My God, my God, why have You forsaken me?"

Thérèse took six months to die, increasingly agonized by the tuberculosis that tore into her body. She had no painkillers; and the treatment offered was almost as painful as the affliction itself. But her physical suffering was as nothing compared with her spiritual desolation. Three months before she died, she said, "Do not be troubled, little sisters, if I suffer much and if you see in me, as I have already said to you, no sign of joy at the moment of death. Our Lord really died as a victim of love, and see what His agony was." Some days later, she returned to the theme of the death of love: "Our Lord died on the Cross in anguish, and yet His was the most beautiful death of love. To die of love does not mean to die in transports. I tell you frankly, it appears to me that this is what I am experiencing."

Thérèse was the master of the spiritual sound-bite. She wrote a note to one of the priests for whom she prayed: "'I am not dying; I am entering into life."

Congreve tells a similar tale, not of himself, but of "a noble and generous spirit", the foundress of a great religious community, who, though loved and honoured to the end, tasted when her working days were over a like experience of a great forsaking, a sense of the loss of all power, opportunity, influence. Coming to her latest days she found them absolutely empty of all that had made her long life exceptionally successful, brimful of interest and hope. She sent for me to tell me of this extraordinary experience of emptiness and forsaking. It was a story of what others would have regarded as a final catastrophe, the failure of a whole life's anticipations; but she told it, I do not say with edifying resignation, but with a face radiant with joy, and the voice with which one tells the best possible news. It was like the transparent and vigorous joy of a very happy child. We were alone, and this was what she confided to me as the result of the complete breakdown of a wonderfully strenuous and influential life: She was nobody now, she had nothing, could be of no use to anyone, was forgotten; and thus she summed it all up: "I think when you have lost everything you have in the world as I have, such a wonderful new life comes into you." It needed the daylight to die, and night to fall, before the stars could appear.

This letting-go is, of course, the nub of the Little Way of Spiritual Childhood which Thérèse enjoined on her readers. In describing it, she made her own remarks about old age. In Chapter 10 of *The Story of a Soul*, she once again remarks that she would like to be a saint:

> You know it has ever been my desire to become a Saint, but I have always felt, in comparing myself with the Saints, that I am as far removed from them as the grain of sand, which the passer-by tramples underfoot, is remote from the mountain whose summit is lost in the clouds.

Instead of being discouraged, I concluded that God would not inspire desires which could not be realised, and that I may aspire to sanctity in spite of my littleness. For me to become great is impossible. I must bear with myself and my many imperfections; but I will seek out a means of getting to Heaven by a little way — very short and very straight, a little way that is wholly new. We live in an age of inventions; nowadays the rich need not trouble to climb the stairs, they have lifts instead. Well, I mean to try and find a lift by which I may be raised to God, for I am too tiny to climb the steep stairway of perfection. I have sought to find in Holy Scripture some suggestion as to what this lift might be which I so much desired, and I read these words uttered by the Eternal Wisdom Itself: "Whosoever is a little one, let him come to Me." Then I drew near to God, feeling sure that I had discovered what I sought; but wishing to know further what He would do to the little one, I continued my search and this is what I found: "You shall be carried at the breasts and upon the knees; as one whom the mother caresses, so will I comfort you."

Never have I been consoled by words more tender and sweet. Your Arms, then, O Jesus, are the lift which must raise me up even to Heaven. To get there I need not grow; on the contrary, I must remain little, I must become still less. O my God, You have gone beyond my expectation, and I . . . "I will sing Your mercies! You have taught me, O Lord, from my youth and till now I have declared Your wonderful works, and thus to old age and grey hairs."

What will this old age be for me? It seems to me that it could as well be now as later: two thousand years are no more in the

Eyes of the Lord than twenty years . . . than a single day! But do not think, dear Mother, that your child is anxious to leave you, and deems it a greater grace to die in the morning rather than in the evening of life; to please Jesus is what she really values and desires above all things.

The way of spiritual childhood is that letting-go of self which comes with old age. But we are not all so strong in the face of pain as the heroic young Carmelite. And, for my part, I find some consolation in the apprehension of what may be to come in the reflections of the aged Fr Congreve. He wrote to his sister, Selina, who was a sister of the Community of St John the Baptist at Clewer, about his increasing old age:

I find growing old something quite new and a surprise. It is a sort of undressing of the soul for the next and better stage of our journey. I am so sure of the purpose of God for us, an increasing purpose from good to better, that I determine not to notice even in my thoughts (if I can help it) the inconveniences and absurdities, mortifications that come with years. *We are not at home in them*, only pushing on through them on the way home … we cannot *like* the discomforts, but we can welcome Christ on our cross - and there is joy in the fellowship of Christ, even when it is a fellowship of suffering.

Congreve went on to explore the nature and use of pain. "Pain shuts the soul up in itself; there is the soul alone with its enemy, the pain. And no word, no bitter cry conveys to the nearest and kindest the reality of what is endured within that solitude." The only way of endurance he finds, then, is to bear it in Christ, for it becomes then "the suffering of two persons supporting one another in love." "It is like a sacrament," he adds, admitting the sufferer into the Sacred Heart of Christ to share the mystery of His voluntary suffering to save the world. In the end there can be only one possible prayer, 'Thy will be done'. With that prayer really said, then suffering is no longer mere pain but God Himself in the pain and God is love.

The value of suffering, he writes, lies "not in the heaviness with which it presses, but in the love with which it is accepted, carried and offered to the eternal Father. 'Lord, do not take me from my cross, only remember me suffering on it.' " And a man's suffering united with the Passion of Christ "cannot stop at his own soul's purifying and profiting, it reaches further to bless and enrich the whole body of the faithful. 'I fill up that which is behind in the sufferings of Christ'."

So often those who are old try and hang on to the things of this world, and then their passing is terrible for them and for those round them. To some extent we all try and cling on. Our two guides, old and young, teach us what Jesus taught: that our true treasure is in heaven; and, old or young, it is not too soon to give up what we hold here to reach for that eternal treasure.

3 Nature and Beauty

On September 8th 1897, the seventh anniversary of her profession and three weeks before her death, the dying Thérèse was surrounded by flowers, which she especially loved. She said, "This is because of God's goodness towards me. Exteriorly I am surrounded by flowers, but interiorly I am always in my trial; however, I am at peace!" She wove some of the flowers into a garland to place by the image of Our Lady of the Smile.

Although she is almost always shown with roses in her hands and is known as "The Little Flower", there is not that much directly about nature in the writings of Thérèse. Flowers and beauty form a backdrop to everything; an unspoken truth about the love of God is that the world is full of beauty. She says that she had expected on entering the Carmel to give up the flowers whose enjoyment had been a great part of her childhood, but that, because so many flowers were sent into the convent, she was always surrounded by them. She remarked that the Bridegroom was always sending his fiancée bouquets.

But, as always in reading Thérèse, there is more than just the supposedly sentimental. In Chapter VI of *The Story of a Soul*, she describes the pilgrimage to Italy that the family joined when she was a child:

> Before reaching the Eternal City, the goal of our pilgrimage, we were given the opportunity of contemplating many marvels. First, there was Switzerland with its mountains whose summits were lost in the clouds, its graceful waterfalls gushing forth in a thousand different ways, its deep valleys literally covered with gigantic ferns and scarlet heather. Ah! Mother, how much

good these beauties of nature, poured out in such profusion, did my soul. They raised it to heaven, which was pleased to scatter such masterpieces on a place of exile destined to last only a day. I hadn't eyes enough to take in everything. Standing by the window I almost lost my breath; I would have liked to be on both sides of the carriage. When turning to the other side, I beheld landscapes of enchanting beauty, totally different from those under my immediate gaze.

At times, we were climbing a mountain peak, and at our feet were ravines the depths of which our glance could not possibly fathom. They seemed about to engulf us. A little later, we were passing through a ravishing little village with its graceful cottages and its belfry over which floated immaculately white clouds. There was, farther on, a huge lake gilded by the sun's last rays, its calm waters blending their azure tints with the fires of the setting sun. All this presented to our enraptured gaze the most poetic and enchanting spectacle one could possibly imagine. And at the end of the vast horizon, we perceived mountains whose indistinct contours would have escaped us, had not their snowy summits made visible by the sun not come to add one more charm to the beautiful lake that thrilled us so.

When I saw all these beauties, very profound thoughts came to life in my soul. I seemed to understand already the grandeur of God and the marvels of heaven. The religious life appeared to me exactly as it is with its subjections, its small sacrifices carried out in the shadows. I understood how easy it is to become all wrapped up in self, forgetting entirely the sublime goal of one's calling. I said to myself: When I am a prisoner in Carmel and trials come my way and I have only a tiny bit of the starry heavens to contemplate, I shall remember what my eyes have seen today. This thought will encourage me and I shall easily forget my own little interests, recalling the grandeur and power of God, this God whom I want to love alone. I shall not have the misfortune of snatching after straws, now that "my HEART HAS AN IDEA of what Jesus has reserved for those who love him."

George Congreve, too, was a man whose spirituality dwelt profoundly on the things of nature. Again and again, growing things and the vistas of the scenery in which he ministered come to the fore in his writings. In nature he found beauty; and in beauty he found God. He was never satisfied to see nature as an end in itself; always nature points us to God, and the only proper response to the beauty of nature is to go beyond the created thing to adore the Creator:

> Separated from God the beauty of nature shuts us in silently. We have no means of communication through it to that which is beyond. The sun-set appears to mean great things; we question it, but it gives no answer; it fades and leaves us the prisoners of silence and darkness. But turning to God in prayer, we find in God all its meaning, and we are set free.

Congreve wrote extensively on beauty in what is really a Christian aesthetic. And if Thérèse did not write aesthetics, she would, I think, have recognized what Congreve was saying. In his sermon on *Beauty*, Congreve says that the sensualist, in his embrace of beauty as a means of pleasure, and the puritan, in his rejection of it as a distraction, both view beauty in essentially the same way. To them beauty "will be like the rose petal to the rose worm, something made for it to curl itself up in and feed upon in its glorious self-complacency. It signifies to him one element in his comfort and convenience, nothing more."

Theology, on the other hand, understands beauty as a sign of the presence of God. Because the Father is the source of all being, He is the source of all beauty. We see the beauty of the Father revealed in Christ, for He is the image (Congreve uses the word "outshining") of the Father's Glory: "As the Catholic Church teaches that God is the vital force which grasps and moves the universe in every atom, so she teaches us also that the Second Person of the Blessed Trinity is the beauty of it."

Failure to see God in beauty comes from failure to understand this true nature; "for want of better teaching, beauty will often mean nothing more than the pattern of a silk or of a wall paper. But here there will be another, whose eyes are opened, who finds beauty everywhere. It carries a message from God to him and he rises with reverence to hear what the Lord God will say to him by it." Congreve goes on:

> We learn also that beauty in any creature is not the creature itself, the sum of its chemical constituents, with colouring, matter or any persistent quality attached to it; the beauty proves to be something emanating from it, transcendent, spiritual, a light which surprises the soul, a sign from heaven, which comes and disappears again, and calls us on to God Who spoke by it. So S. Paul teaches that "every creature is good ... if it be received with thanksgiving, for it is sanctified by the Word of God and prayer." The touch of beauty is not a call to us from God to stay where we are and enjoy our surroundings; it is God's call awakening the soul, summoning it to rise above every creature, and to pass in the Spirit into the presence of God Himself, the King in His beauty, by prayer and praise. A merely sensual delight in beauty stops in the pleasure of the created form, and, having exhausted it, turns wearily to look for another equally disappointing satisfaction.

In the transitoriness of beauty we are constantly reminded of its true significance. When it is recognised as a call from God, its office is accomplished; the soul has seen and understood; it rises up empty, poor, and joyful to go on to Him Who sent the sign. You are aware of the mysterious flash of beauty in some phrase of Music and before you can analyse it, it is gone. You may play the same passage over a hundred times and never recover the first surprise, the revelation it once made to feeling. It is the old mystery of "the lost chord": the magic just touched you and passed back to God from Whom it came; but the beauty of God which it signified is eternal. Created beauty will always be our disappointment, as long as we use it to fill our need of beauty. Rise up, offer it in sacrifice of thanksgiving, follow the delight of it without regret as it passes away from you to God, and in that sacrifice, that parting with the created satisfaction, you raise your will to God, and faith reaches the uncreated Beauty in your praise, You discover the highest significance of beauty as you learn the habit of passing by means of it beyond it, to God Himself, by your act of faith. And now that it is gone, you have not lost it, because in your thanksgiving you followed it on into the presence of God, Who is Himself the Substance and Source of all beauty…

The man of faith reverently gives thanks for the beauty of the world; it is to him a token of a hidden beauty revealed only to a higher kind of sight, the gift of faith, which contemplates the invisible. He does not strain the senses to follow God through the fading beauty of nature; he closes them and waits restfully for the uncreated Glory to rise and look into his spirit. The Kingdom of God is within him.

Thérèse wrote that she would never forget, when she was six or seven, being taken to Trouville and the impression the sea made on her: "I couldn't take my eyes off its majesty, the roaring of its waves, everything spoke to my soul of God's grandeur and power." The Kingdom of God was within her.

I want to leave the last word to Fr Congreve. His meditation, *The Sorrow of Nature*, is a letter he wrote to his nephew Walter, who was serving in the Boer War, from the island off the coast near Cape Town, famous to us as a high-security prison that once held President Nelson Mandela and that long before had been a leper colony. It is for me one of the greatest things Congreve wrote and I am almost always moved to tears when I read it. It profoundly describes how a soul might be moved from the things of this world to a union with God. That desire for complete union with God we share, though we might be divided in other ways. May the vision of its beauty here in the world that we see in our Churches at the Eucharist, and all the beauty of the world, lead us to come to receive Christ in our hearts and come to perfect union with God in Him.

The Sorrow of Nature

Fr George Congreve SSJE

4 The Sorrow of Nature: A Letter written on Robben Island

From The Spiritual Order, Chapter VI - George Congreve SSJE, Longmans & Co., London, 1905

We are keeping here our annual retreat of three days, and this is an ideal place for it. In our Mission it is never easy, even for a few hours, to get quite away from parish cares; it is all the happier when the retreat comes, a gift from heaven, and sets us in such a solitude as this. Here are three full days in which we can taste silence. No talk, no newspaper; but the prayer of the longing of nature on the sea and in the sky, and the human prayer of silence in the heart, and before the altar of the church, which is always open.

After this evening's address on the Passion of our Lord - (it was a tender and reverent recollection of the Mysteries of the last week of His life on earth, and of His glorious death) I went out along up the white road that leads to the Light-house. I made haste in hope to catch a last glimpse of sunset, for though the western horizon was hidden by the rising ground, there was a reflected glow that told of it, high up in a sky clear as crystal, crossed by a few calm lines of closely-reefed violet cloud. But by the time I reached the highest point of the island, whence you can see the whole circle of the sea, the fire was gone out in the west, and there remained only a solemn remembrance of a glory departed. Darkness was falling fast now from the heights above, and only the faintest clouds marked the horizon. One jewel hung over the sea in the clear blue darkness – the evening star; and halfway up the heavens there was the keen crescent of the moon, just beginning to drop low enough to make a ghostly road of silver from the shore to the furthest rim of ocean.

While I stood there a flight of curlews passed me with their wild cry, out of the dark into the dark. The sea made its perpetual moan, uttering the burden of the endless sorrow of a world that cannot rest until man is restored to God. I was conscious of this sorrow of the world everywhere – in the lingering traces of a glory departed in the west, in the cry of the wild birds, and in the voices of the sea far off and near. But I knew that sorrow can never be the whole meaning of nature. With all the solemnities of the close of day out at sea, there falls a majestic sadness everywhere; but why do I submit to its influence, and seek the fellowship of its pain? Why do I listen so hungrily to catch the burden of the breaking waves? To drink the sorrow of the fading light, and the passion of the evening star? Who ever turned to sorrow for sorrow's sake? I find that there is always woven into the sorrow of nature a joyful mystery, which, if it is ever named by men, is called beauty, or love, or praise. If I strain my ear to listen to the sorrow of the sea, it calls me far away from myself, and all this is base, on into the sphere of the infinite, to hear the music of eternity. If I gaze upon the solemnity of the sky at sunset, the pathos is too deep for me: it seems to be the silent marshalling of the heavenly hosts setting the night watch where Love sleeps in a new tomb hewn out of the rock – Love, who is the Light of men. The stillness of the evening clouds expressed for me the patience of the creature waiting for God: "My soul waiteth still upon God."[1] The solitude of the evening star has the beauty of Love left alone in the darkness which fell upon Calvary. The moon's ghostly white track across the sea is the spiritual way of the soul that will dare to follow Jesus Christ, walking on the sea of the world's sorrow, leaving a path of light through the darkness to God. In every sorrowful thing in nature I find the joyful mystery, the uncreated beauty that changes sorrow into joy, - The Son of God in the Sacred Passion, clothing Himself with the our sorrow and offering to the Father His own sorrow with ours, changed into love and praise.

---

[1] Psalm 62.1

As I stand here at night-fall, with the voices of the sea all round me, everything seems to be absorbed in the solemnity of divine mysteries, everything seems awake to the infinite, and to breather the awfulness of eternity. And the mystic bridge by which we pass from the emptiness of our individual solitude to communion with the infinite, we give to it the name "Beauty of the creature."[2] Here God visibly touches nature. This is his sign. By the surprise of the joy of beauty God summons us. We rise and stand upon our feet to hear what He is saying to us, as our hearts burn, and nature at His touch acquires strange significance, sympathy, elevation. At such a time we stand before God in the prayer of silence; we wait for no new call; it is the Lord Himself who is coming; all created things are forgotten; we prepare to receive the Uncreated Loveliness.[3]

Is not something like that the meaning of the fascination of nature – of the love and the fear we have of it? Is not that the reason why I *must* turn and look towards the horizon where the traces of sunset are fading with such solemnity, and why I cannot help listening for the sorrow of the sea breaking along the shore? This lofty and mysterious sadness in things is the point where they transcend themselves, and reach the infinite. The beauty of the creature begins just where it eludes your observation and pursuit. You are conscious that it calls you to rise and follow further out of yourself than you dare, on towards the infinite, invisible Perfection. I have seen, I have heard something which I cannot tell to any one, which is gone, but which has left me more unsatisfied with myself than ever; something, too, which I fear, for it bids me forsake myself and follow the Uncreated Beauty to its home in the heart of God.

---

[2] Cf. St Thomas Aquinas, *In divinis nominibus*, c.4, lect. 5, n. 337

[3] Cf. Louis of Blois, *Oratory of the Faithful Soul*; or, *Devotions to the Most Holy Sacrament, and to Our Blessed Lady*: *Saturday*; also Frederick W. Faber, Cong. Orat., *The Holy Trinity*, from *Hymns*, Burns & Oates, London, 1849; and F. W. Faber, *The Infant God*, Chapter 5 of *Bethlehem*, Thomas Richardson & Son, London, 1860, p.294

And then I find besides, that the sorrow of nature has its strange fascination for me *because its sorrow is my own sorrow.* The whole creation groaneth and travaileth *together*[4]. The news which the cable brought me last week – my own daily moral and spiritual failures and disappointments – I find that the sea carries these sorrows of mine. The clouds know my secret, and hide me and my sorrow in their caverns. And that is part of the mystery of their beauty, which is but a name for love. For the pain which I could not tell to any one even in my community, I heard the sea sorrowing for it. And my delight which I could not share with any friend, however kind he may be, the evening star shone with it in the silent fellowship of my joy.

But what is this sympathetic beauty which I find in nature, this love by which it seems to me to have immortal life, and to find a way into the very centre of the hearts of men? I am sure that whatever power nature may have, it has not only from God originally, but in God also, from moment to moment. The secret of the sympathetic power of nature is the mystery of the Incarnation; Nature in all its forms is an utterance of the Word of God, not merely as He dwelt from all eternity in the unity of the Blessed Trinity, but of the Word made flesh, of Him Who is the outshining of the glory of God, and Who once lay a new-born helpless Child in the straw at Bethlehem. When "the gentleness of heaven is on the sea,"[5] I know why it is so lovely, and whence gentleness comes to us in nature. Nature's secrecy, the character of mystery which haunts it, is a reflexion of the infinite Person from Whom it has its being and destiny. In the vast silence and gloom of nightfall at sea I find the fellowship in sorrow of a world fallen from God, and its yearning to return to the lost fellowship of His Kingdom. When I hear all the waves of the sea mourn for man, that is no feigned

---

[4] Romans 8.22

[5] Cf. William Wordsworth, *By the Sea*, 1802 ("It is a beauteous evening, calm and free")

conceit of affected phrase for me. If I am in Christ, nature really shares my sorrows and mourns with me, because God in Christ girt creation to Himself, and bore the sins and pains of the whole world in His breaking heart upon the cross. The sympathy which I find in nature is the pulse of the heart of the true Mourner for the world's sin – the heart of Him Who carried all our sorrows.[6]

Every precious and lovely thing in nature that I feel or learn, comes to me in some way through the sacrifice of Christ, and has ennobling association with the sorrow that saved the world. And this island is a sanctuary of the sorrows of Christ. Here are detained until they die, apart from their families and friends on the mainland, more than five hundred lepers; here are besides, three or four hundred lunatics, and some seventy coloured convicts working out their penance. The island is a prison, but the Prisoner is Christ, the stricken and afflicted Man Who has no form of outward beauty, rejected of men, the Man of Sorrows, acquainted with grief.[7] One morning I was allowed to kneel with the lepers to receive the holy Sacrament in their church. Here was Mount Calvary, and Christ suffering upon the cross in the person of His stricken members. Hence in retreat on the Lepers' Island we hear the *magnum carmen*[8] of nature in clearer tones than elsewhere. The voices of the sea make their perpetual appeal here for the sorrows of these faithful sufferers, which Christ in them continually offers to the Father. There is a sensible consecration of the island by the sympathetic beauty and sorrow of nature here. Go softly along this shore, for Christ suffers and mourns here. The winds and the sea know it. The sunrise and the sunset know it. Their noble sadness, their undying aspiration, is their fellowship in the suffering and in the victory of Him who clothed Himself with created nature in order to bring it back to God. Is my sin part of

---

[6] Isaiah 53.4
[7] Isaiah 53.3
[8] St Augustine of Hippo, *Letters*, 138.1.5

the burden of humanity for which the lepers suffer? The sorrow of the sea unites with my appeal for them, and mourns with me for the sin. And to-morrow the sunrise and all happy things in the island will praise God with us for the victory of love through pain, and for the hope of that morning (it often comes to one and another prisoner here), which brings for ever the end of sorrow and sin.

The Stations of the Cross

with Fr George Congreve SSJE

compiled by Luke Miller,
Archdeacon of Hampstead

The meditations for the Stations are largely from papers in *The Spiritual Order, with other papers and addresses written for the most part in South Africa*, Longmans, London 1905. The name of the paper from which each quotation is taken and the page in the book are given at the end of each station.

At each station the quotation from Congreve is shown in a paragraph in plain type. Any comment to apply it to the station has been written by Fr Miller and is given in *italics*.

Introductory Prayers

+ In the Name of the Father, and of the Son, and of the Holy Spirit. Amen.

May God, our strength and salvation, be with you all.
And with your spirit.

The Lord said, "No one who does not carry his cross and come after Me can be My disciple." So let us enter into the mysteries His suffering and death, that we may know His forgiveness for our sin, come to be reconciled with Him on His way through death to new life, and enter into the joy of the Kingdom of the Father.

Let us pray.
God of power and mercy, in love You sent Your Son that we might be cleansed of sin and live with You forever. Bless us as we walk in his steps and reflect on His suffering and death, that we may learn from his example the way we should go.
Amen.

> **At the Cross, her station keeping,**
> **Stood the mournful Mother weeping,**
> **Close to Jesus at the last;**
> **Through her soul of joy bereaved,**
> **Bowed with anguish, deeply grieved,**
> **Now at length the sword hath passed.**

> *Stabat Mater dolorosa,* Jacopone da Todi, 13th century

I The Judgement

We adore You, O Christ, and we bless You.
Because by Your holy Cross You have redeemed the world.

The vices which flourished in the decadence of the Roman Empire infect us still. Society, trade, literature, art, even religion, have each its own tendency to observe lying vanities, and breed corruption, so far as in those spheres men construct life for themselves on any principle which leaves no room for God, which dispenses with the being and glory of God. Personal sin implies that God is forsaken for some creature that is loved and worshipped instead of God. Sin in trade implies that there is nothing in the world so important as money. Corruption of art and literature implies that the Divine ideal is forgotten or deliberately shut out, and the creature becomes its own ideal. Here is the essence of idolatry, of false worship; it takes the creature out of its true place, sets it in a false relation, uses it in its emptiness to hide the ghastly absence of God, so as to make life seem interesting enough, dignified enough for the moment, without God.

George Congreve, from *Vanity*, in *The Spiritual Order*, p. 132

Pilate, the creature, judges his Maker, for he has loved power and success in this world instead of God. Here is the essence of idolatry; it takes the creature out of its true place.

We offer this station for those who administer justice and power, and that we may be channels from the Source of the life we have received.

Our Father. Hail Mary. Glory be.

Lord Jesus, crucified,
Have mercy on us.

> **O that blessed one, grief-laden,**
> **Blessed Mother, blessed Maiden,**
> **Mother of the All-holy One;**
> **O that silent, ceaseless mourning,**
> **O those dim eyes, never turning**
> **From that wondrous, suffering Son.**

II Jesus Receives the Cross

We adore You, O Christ, and we bless You.
Because by Your holy Cross You have redeemed the world.

> The wonder which changes life is God's personal interest and
> delight in you, which is incomprehensible to you, and beyond
> natural belief, because you have not deserved it… there you
> find the meaning of the cares of life; you have them all to
> share with Christ, - not because He is so strong that He does
> not care what burdens are thrown upon Him, but because
> He is the eternal Love, and cares for you, whom He made for
> Himself; and to share your sorrow, and carry you and your
> sorrow is to Him no trifle indeed, as the Cross shows you, but
> His delight. Think of this infinite treasure of Love to be found
> in every worry.
> George Congreve, from *Of the Love of God*, in *The Spiritual
> Order*, pp. 352-3

*To share your sorrow, and carry you and your sorrow is to Him no
trifle indeed, as the Cross shows you, but His delight. The cross your
delight: but O my Lord, how sorry I am that you had to bear it for me.*

*We offer this station for those who are afflicted alone with burdens,
and that we may face adversity when it comes and carry our cross
with Christ.*

Our Father. Hail Mary. Glory be.

Lord Jesus, crucified,
Have mercy on us.

Who, on Christ's dear Mother gazing
In her trouble so amazing,
Born of woman would not weep?
Who, on Christ's dear Mother thinking,
Such a cup of sorrow drinking,
Would not share her sorrow deep?

III Jesus Falls the First Time, under the weight of the Cross

We adore You, O Christ, and we bless You.
Because by Your holy Cross You have redeemed the world.

Let us examine ourselves about that which exhausts our life, that by which our life is overstrained. Of course we may make it heavier still by want of order and discipline, but the root of the evil is our separation in heart and will from Christ. The Lord's remedy for the overstrain of our life is not "arrange your work better," or "work harder," or "give up your holiday." No! but "Come unto me and *I* will give you rest;" I will restore freshness to the worried soul and spirit: "Take My yoke upon you, and learn of Me; for I am meek and lowly in heart: and ye shall find rest unto your souls." *There* is our spirits' bath of rejuvenescence and refreshment, the only sphere of perfect relief from care and fretting – in the Heart of Jesus Christ. The body will still be at work, and the mind at full stretch of attention to duty, but the heart, the spirit of the man, his faculty of love and loyalty, will be at rest, for he is no longer alone in anything, but at home in the heart of Jesus Christ where all his responsibilities are shared, his fears laid down.
George Congreve, from *Work and Worry*, in *The Spiritual Order*, pp. 285-6

Remember His words: I go on working and my Father goes on working. (John 5:17) To give us rest, Jesus was laid down in the dust; to take away our fretting and our exhaustion He was exhausted of all things for us.

We offer this station for those who have lapsed from the sacraments, and in penitence for those occasions when we have caused others to fall.

Our Father. Hail Mary. Glory be.

Lord Jesus, crucified,
Have mercy on us.

> **For His people's sins in anguish**
> **There she saw the Victim languish,**
> **Bleed in torments, bleed and die;**
> **Saw the Lord's Anointed taken,**
> **Saw her Child in death forsaken,**
> **Heard His last expiring cry.**

IV Jesus meets His Mother Mary

We adore You, O Christ, and we bless You.
Because by Your holy Cross You have redeemed the world.

> God is infinite, we are each of us nothing; how can the Infinite find room to work in this nothing? It was by the operation of the Holy Ghost, Who is also called the Power of the Highest, that the Humanity of Christ was conceived of the Virgin Mary. There are no limits to the power of His working, except the limits which the free will of man opposes by grieving or quenching His saving energy.
> George Congreve, *The Spiritual Order*, p. 2

Mary, sinless herself, is the symbol of the limitation which God has taken upon Himself for all the children of Eve. The Passion is simply the latest and most explicit moment in the Incarnation; she who laid Him on the wood of the manger will see Him now laid on the wood of the Cross. The Infinite, by the operation of the Holy Spirit, uses His omnipotence to work salvation in the nothingness which is me.

We offer this station for the work of the Holy Places in the Land of Walsingham, England's Nazareth, and for all who watch over us in our struggles as we rely on the power of the Cross we carry in order to follow Christ.

Our Father. Hail Mary. Glory be.

Lord Jesus, crucified,
Have mercy on us.

In the Passion of my Maker
be my sinful soul partaker;
may I bear with her my part,
of His Passion bear the token
in a spirit bowed and broken,
bear His Death within my heart.

V Jesus is Helped by Simon of Cyrene

We adore You, O Christ, and we bless You.
Because by Your holy Cross You have redeemed the world.

> The Saint has nothing, knows nothing, loves nothing, but that he may give it for Christ's sake to whoever wants it: and his store is never exhausted, for the love with which he gives his best thoughts and best works to every one, keeps the spring of his heart always full. You see this in him when he hears of his friend's virtue or success, and he himself has failed; for the honour of Christ he rejoices cordially in the other's success.
>
> George Congreve, *All Saints*, from *The Spiritual Order*, p. 111

"He hears of his friend's virtue or success, and he himself has failed." Jesus in His failure, in stooping under the weight of the Cross such that He needs our help, gives Simon - gives us - the opportunity of virtue. He gives us a chance of offering Him something, who needs nothing. "In so far as you did it to the least of these, you did it to me."

We offer this station for all voluntary aid workers and carers, and for our willingness by Christ to live for others in need and distress.

Our Father. Hail Mary. Glory be.

Lord Jesus, crucified,
Have mercy on us.

May His Wounds both wound and heal me,
He enkindle, cleanse, anneal me;
Be His cross my hope and stay.
May He, when the mountains quiver,
From the flame which burns for ever
Shield me on the Judgement Day.

VI Veronica wipes the Face of Jesus

We adore You, O Christ, and we bless You.
Because by Your holy Cross You have redeemed the world.

There is an idea of life that it is to be comparatively short, but that, while it lasts, it must be a life of iron bondage, a life of labour, exhausting, perhaps menial and humiliating, but to be rewarded in another world by eternal rest. This is not the Christian ideal.

The eternal rest of the blessed is to begin already *here*, and to be fashioned like the finest art work of the master in metals by the blow, and the sculpture, of a laborious life. The metal-master bends over his work and labours all day in the heat and noise of the furnace; but in the midst of all this he has the delight of seeing the hard, dead iron come to life under his hand and put forth branch and leaf and flower.

So think of refreshment, not as something *separate* from all the experience of your daily drudgery, but as a delight sown *in* the daily drudgery by the grace of Christ, and developing into beauty by the very pressure of the burden the dullness of the details.
George Congreve, *Work and Worry*, from *The Spiritual Order*, pp. 279 – 80

Veronica brought refreshment not from the terrible drudgery of the way of the cross, but in the midst of it. Her love made the beauty of Christ visible, and her action of love made her beautiful. So, in the forge of His passion, Christ had the refreshment of seeing the hard, dead iron of her soul come to life under His hand and put forth branch and leaf and flower.

We offer this station for all who care for the sick, weary and dejected, and that we may reflect the blessings and peace that come from the Face of Christ.

Our Father. Hail Mary. Glory be.

Lord Jesus, crucified,
Have mercy on us.

> **Jesus, may Thy cross defend me**
> **And Thy saving death befriend me,**
> **Cherished by Thy deathless grace.**
> **When to dust my dust returneth,**
> **Grant a soul that for Thee yearneth**
> **In Thy paradise a place.**

VII Jesus Falls a Second Time, under the weight of the Cross

We adore You, O Christ, and we bless You.
Because by Your holy Cross You have redeemed the world.

> What does the idea of honour suggest to the Christian? Always what Christ upon the heavenly throne and living in our hearts, suggests. Christ in us is our honour; honour will therefore mean for us nothing strained, affected or dramatic, but simple truth in the inward parts, personal loyalty in our response to God's call of duty, simple generosity, self-sacrifice, and love of the highest. We cannot simulate honour; no external accomplishment can decorate us with this quality; we can only have the highest honour by having the fountain of honour springing up alive within our hearts, and that is Christ on the throne of heaven.
>
> George Congreve, *Honour*, from *The Spiritual Order*, p. 298

Our honour is Christ on the throne of heaven; but my dishonour sent Him sprawling in the dust, despised and rejected, so that my honour might be restored.

We offer this station for those who do not recognise their sins that dishonour our calling from Christ, and that we may know our need of God, be ready to receive the bestowal of God's forgiveness.

Our Father. Hail Mary. Glory be.

Lord Jesus, crucified,
Have mercy on us.

At the Cross, her station keeping,
Stood the mournful Mother weeping,
Close to Jesus at the last;
Through her soul of joy bereaved,
Bowed with anguish, deeply grieved,
Now at length the sword hath passed.

VIII Jesus Greets the Women of Jerusalem

We adore You, O Christ, and we bless You.
Because by Your holy Cross You have redeemed the world.

> Happiness in possessing God is by no means reserved to be the final reward of the perfect in a future life. There is not only the crowning grace to be given at last to those who have fought their good fight out, - "Well done … ; enter thou into the joy of the Lord;" but there is also a grace of joy by which we beginners are to encourage one another in entering upon our warfare, and through every day's march. There is the joy of saints who have entered into rest, who never can sin again, never again be tempted; but we who are in temptation every day, we who are penitents, still in *valle lacrymarum* – there is blessedness for us too; we must be "sorrowful yet always rejoicing" – and this joy of penitents is no doubtful or make believe, but the sincerest, most cordial, joy.
>
> George Congreve, *Single-hearted in the Way*, from *The Spiritual Order*, p. 117

'Weep not for me, but for yourselves'. Here in this vale of tears let us be sorrowful for our sins and thus find the way to joy; be sorrowful in the right way that we might be always rejoicing.

We offer this station for all victims of warfare, violence and abuse, as well as those who perpetrate it, and that we may live and work for justice and protection for the afflicted, and peace and harmony in every corner of the world.

Our Father. Hail Mary. Glory be.

Lord Jesus, crucified,
Have mercy on us.

> **O that blessed one, grief-laden,**
> **Blessed Mother, blessed Maiden,**
> **Mother of the All-holy One;**
> **O that silent, ceaseless mourning,**
> **O those dim eyes, never turning**
> **From that wondrous, suffering Son.**

IX Jesus Falls a Third Time, under the weight of the Cross

We adore You, O Christ, and we bless You.
Because by Your holy Cross You have redeemed the world.

The Christian account of creation is that God has made all things very good, nothing in vain, and yet everything incomplete in itself, and all creatures together ineffectual and empty in themselves; and this because His purpose is, *Himself* to become their fullness, that in which they reach their perfection their full meaning. Man represents and sums up all the stages of Creation in himself. Fallen from God, his emptiness is irremediable. But Christ has come to him in his sin to deliver him from the intolerable loneliness and littleness of life separated from God. Christ is the head of the new race, the saved humanity; he is man filled with all the fullness of the Godhead bodily. Brought by the working of the Holy Spirit into union with Him, of His fullness we all receive and grace upon grace.

George Congreve, *The Fullness of God*, from *The Spiritual Order*, p. 24

But to give us of His fullness He was emptied out into the dust. To come to us He had to fall to the lowest place so that He was where we are.

We offer this station for all who have never known the generous, life-fulfilling coming of Christ, and that we may be made worthy to receive his grace to life faithfully in him to the full.

Our Father. Hail Mary. Glory be.

Lord Jesus, crucified,
Have mercy on us.

> **Who, on Christ's dear Mother gazing**
> **In her trouble so amazing,**
> **Born of woman would not weep?**
> **Who, on Christ's dear Mother thinking,**
> **Such a cup of sorrow drinking,**
> **Would not share her sorrow deep?**

X Jesus is Stripped of His Garments

We adore You, O Christ, and we bless You.
Because by Your holy Cross You have redeemed the world.

Congreve invites us to look with the eye of imagination at a sea shell.

The peculiar delicacy of form and tint in this tiny shell links it to that infinite mystery, the mind of Christ, Who is the revelation to man of the beauty of God. The reason of the rare grace of any rock plant, and of the majesty of the mountains and of the cloud world; the reason of the art-mastery of the frost patterns on the window pane; the reason of all these variously beautiful things is one with the Eternal Word of God, as He is One with the Father. "The Eternal Son of God His Word," says a commentator on S Thomas, "is the source of all beauty; He is the beauty which touches all creatures; it is His loveliness we discover in them." As the Catholic Church teaches that God is the vital force which grasps and moves the universe in every atom, so she teaches us also that the Second Person of the Blessed Trinity is the beauty of it.

George Congreve, *Beauty*, from *The Spiritual Order*, pp. 317-8

And He is stripped, and exposed to us, the revelation to man of the beauty of God, made horrible to look upon and exciting in us ugly thoughts of violence and lust. He is stripped.

We offer this station for those who are poor, or homeless or without work and livelihood, and that we may never look on people in need with anything other than the love and help we ourselves have received from God.

Our Father. Hail Mary. Glory be.

Lord Jesus, crucified,
Have mercy on us.

> **For His people's sins in anguish**
> **There she saw the Victim languish,**
> **Bleed in torments, bleed and die;**
> **Saw the Lord's Anointed taken,**
> **Saw her Child in death forsaken,**
> **Heard His last expiring cry.**

XI Jesus is Nailed to the Cross

We adore You, O Christ, and we bless You.
Because by Your holy Cross You have redeemed the world.

As Christian gentleness and peaceableness are tested roughly by what happen to us every day, it is well often to look on the solid ground of our peace, in order that we might be able to stand there when trouble comes. Our peace is not a comfortable consciousness of some spiritual feeling that we may discover in ourselves, nor of some moral improvement that we have made, or of victory over some special fault. If our peace must be sought there, we could never be sure of it. But our peace is the Son of God Himself, taking us one by one, and reconciling us to the Father in Himself. On this account we call it "The peace which passeth all understanding;" God's peace; the quietness of a soul that rests by faith on God. Storms beat upon the house that was built upon the rock and it fell not. The rock is the Divine nature; the Christian's peace is built upon the truth of God Himself, the unmoving centre of the Universe.

George Congreve, *Christ our Peace*, from *The Spiritual Order*, p. 226

As Christian gentleness and peaceableness are tested roughly by what happens to us every day, it is well often to look on the solid ground of our peace: "Father forgive them, for they know not what they do." The Christian's peace is built upon the truth of God Himself, the unmoving centre of the Universe. Upon Christ, held fast by the nails of His love, unmoving upon the cross for our peace and our salvation.

We offer this station for all who suffer from constant pain and in penitence for those occasions when we have hurt others.

Our Father. Hail Mary. Glory be.

Lord Jesus, crucified,
Have mercy on us.

> **In the Passion of my Maker**
> **be my sinful soul partaker;**
> **may I bear with her my part,**
> **of His Passion bear the token**
> **in a spirit bowed and broken,**
> **bear His Death within my heart.**

XII Jesus Dies on the Cross

We adore You, O Christ, and we bless You.
Because by Your holy Cross You have redeemed the world.

From a letter written on Robben Island, off Cape Town.

Every precious and lovely thing in nature that I feel or learn comes to me in some way through the sacrifice of Christ and has ennobling association with the sorrow that has saved the world. And this island is a sanctuary of the sorrows of Christ. Here are detained until they die, apart from their families and friends on the mainland, more than five hundred lepers; here are, besides, three or four hundred lunatics, and some seventy coloured convicts working out their penance. The island is a prison, but the prisoner is Christ, the stricken and afflicted Man Who has no form or outward beauty, rejected of men, Man of Sorrows, acquainted with grief. One morning I was allowed to kneel with the lepers and receive the holy Sacrament in their church. Here was Mount Calvary, and Christ suffering upon the Cross in the person of His suffering members. Hence in retreat on the Lepers' Island we hear the "magnum carmen" of nature in clearer tones than elsewhere. The voices of the sea make their perpetual appeal here for the sorrows of those faithful sufferers, which Christ in them continually offers to the Father. There is a sensible consecration of the island by the sympathetic beauty and sorrow of nature here. Go softly along this shore, for Christ suffers and mourns here. The winds and the sea know it. Their noble sadness, their undying aspiration, is their fellowship in the suffering and in the victory of Him Who clothed Himself with created nature in order to bring it back to God. Is my sin part of the burden of humanity for which the lepers suffer? The sorrow of the sea unites with my appeal for them, and mourns with me for the sin. And tomorrow the sunrise and all happy things in the island will praise God with us for the victory of love through pain, and for the hope of that morning (it often comes to one and another prisoner here), which brings forever the end of sorrow and sin.

George Congreve, *The Sorrow of Nature*, from *The Spiritual Order*, pp. 57-8

Congreve teaches us the unity and equality of all souls in Christ. We are afflicted by sinfulness that we cannot see even in the most profound self-examination: this is the human condition, its sorrow, the original sin of man. But because of the darkness of the Cross, in the sunrise all happy things will praise God for the victory of love through pain, and for the end forever of sorrow and sin.

We offer this station for those who are troubled in spirit or who live with constant weakness or pain, and that we may help them to bear their sorrows and through our love bring hope.

Our Father. Hail Mary. Glory be.

Lord Jesus, crucified,
Have mercy on us.

> **May His Wounds both wound and heal me,**
> **He enkindle, cleanse, anneal me;**
> **Be His cross my hope and stay.**
> **May He, when the mountains quiver,**
> **From the flame which burns for ever**
> **Shield me on the Judgement Day.**

XIII The body of Jesus is Taken Down from the Cross and Laid in the Arms of His Blessed Mother

We adore You, O Christ, and we bless You.
Because by Your holy Cross You have redeemed the world.

Congreve quotes Archbishop Leighton (Archbishop of Glasgow, 1670).

" 'Ye shall weep and lament, but the world shall rejoice: ye shall be sorrowful, but your sorrow shall be turned into joy.' The water of those tears shall be turned into wine of consolation. The traffic of these rivers is gainful; they export grief and import joy. When these tears are called seed, the harvest crop is called joy. 'They that sow in tears shall reap in joy.' They are here called *rivers* and they are answered by a river for which in the end they shall be perfectly exchanged. 'Thou shalt make them drink from the river of Thy pleasures.' 'The Lamb shall feed them and lead them unto living fountains of water.' Here they run down the eyes, and water the cheeks, and there you read that God shall wipe these away from their eyes. Who would not be content to weep to have God wipe away their tears with His own hand? Be ambitious then to be found among the mourners in Zion."
Generous Grief, from *The Spiritual Order*, p. 156

When I am tempted I must remember this moment of grief and be firm in my resolve not to add more to these tears. Christ's death is for the salvation of the world: Mary's tears show us the way: let us cling to Jesus, whom we have killed with our sin, but whose death is our salvation. 'Who would not be content to weep to have God wipe away their tears with His own hand?'

We offer this station for all who mourn and are coping with loss, and that we may be the ones to bring consolation by the joy of hoping in the Lord crucified for our sake Who rose again to new life.

Our Father. Hail Mary. Glory be.

Lord Jesus, crucified,
Have mercy on us.

> **Jesus, may Thy cross defend me**
> **And Thy saving death befriend me,**
> **Cherished by Thy deathless grace.**
> **When to dust my dust returneth,**
> **Grant a soul that for Thee yearneth**
> **In Thy paradise a place.**

XIV The Body of Jesus is Laid in the Tomb

We adore You, O Christ, and we bless You.
Because by Your holy Cross You have redeemed the world.

From a meditation for a friend who was 89 years old, and who died just a few days after the date of this paper.

Is not the one Good of life to give it to you, O God? My dying to all outward things in old age shall mean my Sacrifice; the free gift of myself, my remembrances, my present, my future, my life and my death, to Thee, Who lovedst me, and gavest Thyself for me. The Sacrifice on the Altar grows less and less as the fire consumes it; and Thou takest to Thyself that which dies to earth. I have given myself often to Thee my God in the Holy Sacrifice of the Altar, and am glad that Thou takest me at my word; I am glad thus to die to myself, to grow less and less, and become nothing to this world, that Christ may become all to me, and that I may belong only to Him.

I am a stranger and a pilgrim here. Let me go that I may depart to my own country.

Meditation for a Friend's 89th Birthday from *The Spiritual Order*, p. 330

It is not recorded when Fr Congreve said his last Mass. Of Fr Benson it is said that he became shaky and the Superior decided that the Fr Founder should no longer go to the altar. His name was simply removed from the rotas. Nothing was said. Benson three days running asked the young Brother who cared for him to go and look at the list; after the third day he never asked again. But in imitation of Christ, death for the Christian is but the completion of the sacrifice, the end of worship in one way and the beginning of a new worship. In death we are still close to Christ for He too died that we might live. 'I am glad thus to die to myself, to grow less and less, and become nothing to this world, that Christ may become all to me, and that I may belong only to Him.' A footnote at the end of this passage reads simply: 'MCL departed this life January 24th 1895 RIP.'

We offer this station for all who have died, and that we may live to Christ in this world, go out to meet him when he comes, take up our cross daily to the moment of our death and thus be happy with him in the world to come.

Our Father. Hail Mary. Glory be.

Lord Jesus, crucified,
Have mercy on us.

> **O sacred Head, sore wounded,**
> **defiled and put to scorn;**
> **O kingly Head, surrounded**
> **with mocking crown of thorn:**
> **What sorrow mars Thy grandeur?**
> **Can death Thy bloom deflower?**
> **O countenance Whose splendour**
> **the hosts of heaven adore!**
>
> **Thy beauty, long-desirèd,**
> **hath vanished from our sight;**
> **Thy power is all expirèd,**
> **and quenched the Light of light.**

Ah me! for whom Thou diest,
hide not so far Thy grace:
show me, O Love most highest,
the brightness of Thy Face.

I pray thee, Jesus, own me,
me, Shepherd good, for Thine;
Who to Thy fold hast won me,
and fed with truth divine.
Me guilty, me refuse not,
incline Thy face to me,
this comfort that I lose not,
on earth to comfort Thee.

In Thy most bitter Passion
My heart to share doth cry,
With Thee for my salvation
Upon the cross to die.
Ah, keep my heart thus moved
To stand Thy cross beneath;
To mourn Thee, Well-Beloved,
Yet thank Thee for Thy death!

Salve caput cruentatum, Arnulf van Leuven, d. 1250, tr. Robert Bridges, 1844-1933

Man of Sorrows! What a name
for the Son of God, who came
ruined sinners to reclaim!
    Alleluia! What a Saviour!
Or in Lent and Holy Week:
    Christus vincit! Christ regnat!

Bearing shame and scoffing rude,
in my place condemned He stood;
sealed my pardon with His blood:
    Alleluia! What a Saviour!

Guilty, helpless, lost were we;
spotless Lamb of God was He:
full atonement - can it be?
    Alleluia! What a Saviour!

Lifted up was He to die;
'It is finished!' was His cry;
now in heaven exalted high:
    Alleluia! What a Saviour!

When He comes, our glorious King,
all His ransomed home to bring,
then anew this song we'll sing:
    Alleluia! What a Saviour!

Philip Bliss, 1838-1876

Concluding Prayers

Lord Jesus Christ, Your passion and death is the sacrifice that unites earth and heaven and reconciles all people to You. May we who have faithfully reflected on these mysteries follow in Your steps and so come to share Your glory in heaven, where You live and reign with the Father and the Holy Spirit one God, for ever and ever. **Amen**.

May the souls of the faithful departed through the mercy of God rest in peace. **Amen.**

May the Divine Assistance remain with us always. **Amen.**

The Catholic League

a Registered Charity in England & Wales, Number 232443
is a society whose four objects are – the promotion of fellowship among Catholic believers – the union of all Christians with the Apostolic See of Rome – the spread of the Catholic faith – the deepening of the spiritual life.

President
The Revd Michael Rear

Priest Director and Editor of The Messenger
The Revd Mark Woodruff
Telephone: 07710 024505   Email: director@unitas.org.uk

General Secretary
David Chapman
293 Ordnance Road, ENFIELD, Middlesex EN3 6HB
Telephone: 01992 763893   Email: secretary@unitas.org.uk

Treasurer
Cyril Wood
13 Merino Green, Oakridge Park, MILTON KEYNES MK14 6FL
Telephone: 01525 375297   Email: thecatholicleague@gmail.com

Director of the Apostolate of Prayer and Membership Secretary
The Revd Christopher Stephenson
27 Moor Lane, Newby, SCARBOROUGH, North Yorkshire YO12 5SL
Telephone: 01732 378572   Email: members@unitas.org.uk

Priest Director of the Sodality of the Precious Blood
The Revd Graeme Rowlands
St Silas' Presbytery, 11 St Silas Place, LONDON NW5 3QP
Telephone: 020 7485 3727